delish
ULTIMATE COCKTAILS

100+
AMAZING
RECIPES
Inside!

delish

ULTIMATE
COCKTAILS

Why Limit Happy to an Hour?

Joanna Saltz & the Editors of Delish

HEARST
HOME

TO THOSE
WHOSE GLASS IS
**ALWAYS
HALF FULL**

CONTENTS

IS IT 5 O'CLOCK YET

MIGHT BE VODKA

THAT'S JO!

DRINK RESPONSIBLY.

I feel the need to say that at the beginning of this book due to the mere fact that we're about to unleash 8 chapters of boozy chaos upon you. It's undeniable that cocktails are at the core of Delish's brand mentality: Our drinks, punches, and crazy shots have been some of our most searched–for and celebrated recipes since we launched five years ago. But I swear that while we've loved creating every single one of them, it's never really been about the excess and alcohol. (Yes, our team has had one too many drinks together. No, I don't want to talk about it.)

What it *is* about is how we're just constantly looking for an excuse to get together—we honestly can't resist. And to prove that point, I asked the team to tell me their most random excuses they've ever found to throw a party. They did **NOT** disappoint:

"We celebrated Kourtney Kardashian being pregnant."

"Someone said that you couldn't play Katy Perry's 'Firework' four times in a row without someone noticing, so we threw a party to test that theory."

"I found money in my old jeans."

"We threw a party for not being pregnant on Mother's Day."

Truthfully, if you're like us, you don't really need this cookbook to get the party started. But making sure you have one of our amazing drinks in your hand when it does would be the truly responsible thing to do.

JO SALTZ
Editorial Director

HOME-BAR ESSENTIALS

A liquor cabinet is never fully dressed without these necessities.

DRY VERMOUTH
A fortified wine that's a MUST for a legit martini. (Get a small bottle; the aromatics fade fast after opening.)

TRIPLE SEC
Do yourself a favor and splurge for Cointreau. It's worth it.

GRENADINE
The same sweet–tart syrup used in Shirley Temples will elevate your grown–up drinks too.

STRAINER
Essential for seamless pouring.

BITTERS
A few dashes here and there in cocktails (or even seltzer, TBH) add major dimension.

SIMPLE SYRUP
Impress your friends with this wildly basic sweetener of equal parts sugar and water.

MARASCHINO CHERRIES
Ditch the candy–red kind for the real deal: Luxardo maraschinos.

MARGARITA SALT
If you're blending margs on the reg, you need this.

SQUARE ICE-CUBE TRAYS
Perfect squares make any cocktail look instantly more legit.

COCKTAIL SHAKER
Chill drinks without ever getting melted ice in your drink.

METAL STRAWS
Reusable and comes rose gold or rainbow? Yes, please!

JIGGER
The only way you'll ever measure your booze again.

MUDDLER
The sturdy bottom means it'll crush mint for mojitos for years.

GIN
Your summer self who wants everything light and fruity will thank you.

VODKA
Forget your memories of college hangovers: This one's a must.

RUM
Necessary for anything tropical—and we know there's always one person who can't resist it.

TEQUILA
For your many blenders of frozen margs.

WHISKEY
Get one decent enough for Dad to sip straight and for you to stir up Manhattans.

COGNAC
A crucial component for classics like the sidecar and Sazerac.

Find this **SPICY GRAPEFRUIT SIDECAR** recipe on page 24!

THE ULTIMATE GUIDE TO GLASSWARE

FLUTE

To keep champagne, prosecco, and cava extra bubbly, you're going to want to use a flute. The small surface up top (due to the narrow taper of the glass) traps the effervescence. I.e., Your mimosa will stay fizzy for longer.

Pair it with: Apple Cider Mimosas, page 72

SHOT GLASS

At its core, the shot glass helps you measure how much booze you're adding to a cocktail. (Most American versions hold between 1.25 and 1.5 fluid ounces.) You can serve festive "shooter" drinks straight out of them too though.

Pair it with: Tiramisu Shots, page 92

HIGHBALL GLASS

The tall highball is a sturdy catchall for ice-filled drinks or ones that are made with a generous amount of mixer. A highball cocktail does exist (it's just booze and club soda), but it's far from the only thing you can pour in this glass.

Pair it with: Sparkling Tequila Sunrise, page 160

MARTINI GLASS

This shape riffs on the original 19th-century all-purpose "cocktail glass." When martinis became popular, the glass grew larger and more conical to accommodate the drink. The sloping sides prevent ingredients from separating, and the large opening allows the alcohol's aroma to surface.

Pair it with: Classic Martini, page 16

HURRICANE GLASS

The hurricane glass earned its name from the hurricane lamp (they have the same shape), and the hurricane cocktail earned its name from the glass. The extra-large body allows for a double serving of rum, which hurricane cocktails call for; nowadays, the glass is a go-to for other fruity blended drinks too.

Pair it with: Blue Hawaiian Coolers, page 144

LOWBALL GLASS

Technically, rocks glasses, old-fashioned glasses, and lowball glasses have niche uses, but novices use the names interchangeably. The lowball is the most general moniker, and the glass is essentially just the highball's shorter cousin. It's great for muddled cocktails or ones that are poured over ice (hence the "rocks" name).

Pair it with: Mojitos, 3 Ways, page 20

COUPE

Before flutes came into favor, people would pour champagne into these shallow, saucer-shaped glasses. But the wide mouth doesn't contain carbonation very well. We like to use them for blended drinks—just because they're pretty.

Pair it with: Strawberry Frose, page 146

MARGARITA GLASS

If a martini glass and a coupe had a baby, you'd get something akin to a margarita glass. It has a wide rim for salt and sugar and a large bowl that can hold plenty of ice.

Pair it with: Classic Margarita, page 40

COPPER MUG

The cold metal of this mug acts as insulation for any chilled ingredients that go inside of it. A Moscow mule is usually served in one, and there's an additional reason for that: Copper can increase the potency of ginger beer's carbonation.

Pair it with: Moscow Mule Punch, page 154

CLASSICS

DONE RIGHT

DON'T OVERTHINK IT!

CLASSIC MARTINI

SERVES 1 | TOTAL TIME: 5 MIN

Shaken—never stirred. A classic martini is beloved for its simplicity: It's just vodka or gin, vermouth, and a lemon peel. These are our ideal ratios. Make it dirty with a splash of olive juice.

Ice

2½ ounces vodka

½ ounce dry vermouth

Green olive (or lemon peels)

1. Place a martini glass in the freezer until chilled, about 15 minutes.

2. Fill a cocktail shaker with ice. Add vodka and vermouth and shake until well chilled. Strain into a martini glass, then garnish with olive or lemon peel.

I like to do some things the old-fashioned way.

SHAKE IT LIKE 007

Once you graduate to a cocktail shaker, you gotta master the technique. Mixing a drink this way chills the liquor, blends your ingredients, and dilutes the booze with just enough ice to make it palatable. Here's how to get your shake on.

• **First, add ice. Fill the shaker halfway with ice to start the cooldown process and make sure your liquids don't overflow.**

• **Then give it a little muscle. And don't be gentle here. Positioning the shaker over your shoulder will ensure you lean into the shake— and make the floor behind you the spot for any spills.**

• **Always use a tight grip. To eliminate drips, make sure you hold both pieces of the shaker super securely while you shake.**

WHITE RUSSIAN

If you're a coffee drinker, these go down a little too easy. They're smooth and creamy, so it's no wonder The Dude from *The Big Lebowski* had one in his hand the entire movie.

Ice

2 ounces Kahlúa

2 ounces vodka

2 ounces heavy cream

1. Fill a rocks glass with ice, then add Kahlúa and vodka.

2. Top with heavy cream.

MAKE IT DESSERT!
Drizzle ½ ounce **chocolate syrup** over **ice** before adding the booze.

MOJITOS, 3 WAYS

SERVES 3 | TOTAL TIME: 20 MIN

No matter your favorite fruit, muddle it with lime juice, sugar, and fresh mint and we can guarantee you'll find summertime bliss. Just add rum.

½ cup lime juice

3 teaspoons granulated sugar, divided

1 bunch fresh mint

¾ cup fruit of choice

Ice

6 ounces white rum

1 (12-ounce) can seltzer

1. Divide lime juice evenly among 3 glasses. To each glass, add a teaspoon of sugar, 2 mint leaves, and ¼ cup fruit. Using the back of a wooden spoon, muddle fruit and mint.

2. Fill each glass two-thirds full with ice cubes. Add 2 ounces rum to each glass and top with seltzer.

3. Garnish with lime slice, mint, and matching fruit.

1

PINEAPPLE MOJITO
Use chopped pineapple in the drink and garnish with a small wedge.

2
—
STRAWBERRY MOJITO
Quarter the strawberries before muddling, but save the prettiest whole strawberries for garnish.

3
—
BLUEBERRY MOJITO
Skewer blueberries onto bamboo cocktail picks to make them look fancy!

ROSEMARY GIN FIZZ

SERVES 1 | TOTAL TIME: 45 MIN

Frothy and bubbly, this elegant cocktail is our NYE go-to. The secret to its creamy top? An egg white, shaken up—and up and up—until it's foamy.

FOR THE ROSEMARY SIMPLE SYRUP:

1 cup water

1 cup granulated sugar

3 sprigs fresh rosemary

FOR THE GIN FIZZ:

2 ounces gin

1 ounce freshly squeezed lemon juice

1 ounce rosemary simple syrup

1 egg white*

Ice

5 ounces seltzer

Lemon sliced, for garnish

Rosemary, for garnish

1. Make rosemary simple syrup: In a small saucepan over medium heat, combine water, sugar, and rosemary. Bring to a boil and stir until all sugar is dissolved. Let cool to room temperature, then strain into an airtight container and refrigerate until ready to use.

2. Make drink: Combine gin, lemon juice, simple syrup, and egg white in a cocktail shaker. Shake for 10 to 15 seconds to combine all ingredients. Fill shaker with ice and shake 10 to 15 seconds more or until chilled.

3. Strain into serving glass, top with seltzer, and garnish with lemon and rosemary.

*Consuming raw eggs may increase your risk of foodborne illness.

**INFUSE
YOUR SIMPLE
SYRUP**
with rosemary to bring
out gin's botanical
notes. Or make
it more summery
with basil.

SPICY GRAPEFRUIT SIDECAR

SERVES 1 | TOTAL TIME: 15 MIN

If the idea of sipping cognac kinda scares you, fear not: This concoction of grapefruit juice and triple sec (which is what makes margs go down so easy) plus a sweet-and-spicy rim is bomb.

Grapefruit wedge, for rimming glasses

2 teaspoons granulated sugar, for rimming glasses

2 teaspoons chili powder, for rimming glasses

Ice

2 ounces cognac

2 ounces grapefruit juice

1 ounce Cointreau

Grapefruit slice, for garnish

1. Rim glass with a grapefruit wedge. Combine sugar and chili powder on a small plate and dip rim into mixture, turning to coat.

2. Fill a cocktail shaker with ice and add cognac, grapefruit juice, and Cointreau. Shake until chilled.

3. Strain into rimmed glass and garnish with a grapefruit slice.

STRAWBERRY DAIQUIRI

SERVES 2 | TOTAL TIME: 15 MIN

The OG daiquiri has just rum, sugar, and fresh lime juice. But since our earliest days of boozin', we've preferred it with strawberries. After a lot of research, we think a mix of fresh and frozen gives it the best texture.

½ cup white rum

½ cup fresh strawberries, chopped

1 (10-ounce) bag frozen strawberries, chopped

Juice of 1 lime

Sliced lime, for garnish

Strawberries, for garnish

1. Add rum, fresh and frozen strawberries, and lime juice to a blender and blend until smooth.

2. Divide between 2 glasses then garnish with lime slices and strawberries.

GIANT MOSCOW MULE

PHD TERRACE, DREAM MIDTOWN NEW YORK, NY

PHD Terrace's massive moscow mule was the cocktail seen 'round the world. Not only did the original version blow up on Instagram, but the bar also dropped an Orange Blossom version in Zola for March's National Moscow Mule Day that went even more viral than its predecessor did.

It was a natural follow-up to the OG Moscow mule, says Matt Strauss, managing partner of the TAO group, as "bigger, and done right, is better." After lots of workshopping, the end result clocked in at 10 pounds, contained an entire bottle of vodka, served up to eight people, and cost... $225. If you do the math, it cost about $28 a person, which, yes, is a little steep for drinks with friends, but (1) it made brunch a whole lot more fun, and (2) you also got the novelty of an Insta-worthy photo moment that would live on forever.

The cocktail is a mix of blood-orange puree and ginger beer, but let's talk garnishes. Notable ones included rock candy, blood-orange foam, and an oversized white-chocolate sphere covered in boozy gummy bears. "Sure, the photo is important," Strauss says, "but it needed to be up to our standards, or we wouldn't have served it." Delish can confirm: The drink was delightful.

While this particular drink likely won't come back anytime soon, Strauss explains it was a "jumping-off point" for bigger and better cocktails. All that is to say, if you like a gigantic vat of craftily put-together alcohol, you might want to hit up PHD Terrace, like, now.

CHERRY SAZERAC

SERVES 1 | TOTAL TIME: 20 MIN

The absinthe rinse—which is a mixologist's way of saying "swirl around liquor in a glass"—is what makes this drink so sophisticated. We keep with tradition but add some fun with a splash of maraschino cherry juice for a bright, fruity finish.

1 ounce absinthe

Ice

1 teaspoon maraschino cherry juice

2 dashes Peychaud's bitters

2 ounces rye whiskey

1 ounce cognac

Lemon peel, for garnish

Maraschino cherry, for garnish

1. Place a cocktail glass in the freezer until chilled, at least 10 minutes. Add absinthe to chilled glass and swirl around. Discard liquid.

2. Fill a mixing glass or cocktail shaker with ice. Add cherry juice, bitters, whiskey, and cognac. Stir until chilled, then strain into cocktail glass.

3. Garnish with a lemon peel and a maraschino cherry.

BROWN SUGAR OLD-FASHIONED

SERVES 1 | TOTAL TIME: 10 MIN

Brown sugar + bourbon = always a good idea. Swapping out the granulated sugar gives this beloved cocktail a molasses-like flavor that tastes kinda like toffee.

1 teaspoon packed brown sugar

1 teaspoon water

2 dashes angostura bitters

2 ounces bourbon

Ice

Orange peel, for garnish

Cinnamon stick, for garnish

1. Add sugar, water, and bitters to glass. Muddle until sugar is dissolved. Add bourbon and ice and stir to combine.

2. Garnish with an orange peel and cinnamon stick.

FROZEN DARK & STORMY

You don't have to wait for sh*tty weather to blend up a batch of these slushies. We add a big spoonful of freshly grated ginger for even more kick.

3 cups ice

1 (12-ounce) can ginger beer

1 tablespoon fresh ginger

Juice of 1 lime

4 ounces dark rum

1. In a blender, combine ice, ginger beer, ginger, and lime juice and blend until smooth.

2. Divide between glasses and float 2 ounces dark rum on top of each.

FROZEN PIMM'S CUP

SERVES 4 | TOTAL TIME: 15 MIN

You don't have to be in the seats at Wimbledon or a polo match to sip on a Pimm's Cup—especially when you turn it into a slushie. The less–proper icy version blends up citrus and a bunch of fresh ginger for some legit zing.

---

4 cups ice

1¼ cups Pimm's No. 1

¾ cups ginger ale

½ cup lemonade

1 tablespoon freshly chopped ginger

FOR THE GARNISH:

Mint leaves

Orange slices

Sliced strawberries

Cucumber ribbons

1. In a large blender, combine ice, Pimm's, ginger ale, lemonade, and ginger and blend until smooth.

2. Pour into glasses and garnish with mint and fruit.

GINGER LIME WHISKEY SOUR

SERVES 1 | TOTAL TIME: 45 MIN

A little classier than a whiskey ginger, but it's still far from complicated. We swap out the lemon juice for lime and infuse freshly grated ginger into simple syrup for a fiery upgrade.

FOR THE SIMPLE SYRUP:

½ cup water

¼ cup granulated sugar

3–inch piece fresh ginger, peeled and thinly sliced

FOR THE WHISKEY SOUR:

Ice

2 ounces bourbon

Juice of 1 lime

2 tablespoons ginger simple syrup

1 egg white*

½–inch piece ginger, for rimming glasses

Lime wedge, for garnish

Maraschino cherry, for garnish

1. Make ginger simple syrup: In a small saucepan over medium heat, combine water, sugar, and ginger. Bring to a boil, stirring to dissolve sugar, and boil 6 minutes. Let cool, then strain using a small spatula to squeeze and press against ginger solids. Discard ginger.

2. Make whiskey sour: Fill a cocktail shaker with ice. Add bourbon, lime juice, simple syrup, and egg white. Shake until chilled.

3. Rim glass with cut ginger. Strain drink into glass and garnish with a lime wedge and cherry.

Consuming raw eggs may increase your risk of foodborne illness.

CLASSIC MAI TAI

SERVES 2 | TOTAL TIME: 10 MIN

Turns on OOO message This famous tiki cocktail is as tropical as it gets. Freshly squeezed orange and lime juice deliver big citrus flavor, but its best ingredient is orgeat syrup (a sweet syrup made from almonds). We like it hot with a spicy rim.

Lime wedge, for rimming glasses

1 tablespoon chili powder, for rimming glasses

2 ounces dark rum

2 ounces white rum

2 ounces orange juice

Juice of 1 lime

2 ounces orange curaçao

1 ounce orgeat syrup

Ice

2 tablespoons grenadine

Pineapple wedges, for garnish

Lime slices, for garnish

Maraschino cherries, for garnish

1. Rim 2 glasses with a lime wedge. Place chili powder on a small plate and dip rim into chili powder, turning to coat.

2. Divide rums, orange juice, lime juice, curaçao, and orgeat syrup between glasses and stir. Fill with ice, then divide grenadine between glasses.

3. Garnish with fruit.

ORGEAT SYRUP can be hard to find in stores. Buy it online or use simple syrup instead.

CLASSIC MARGARITAS

SERVES 2 | TOTAL TIME: 5 MIN

If you ask most Delish staffers what their last meal would be, many would say, "Chips, guac, margarita on the rocks." We've had lots of practice perfecting this ratio of tequila to triple sec to lime juice. Make it spicy by swapping in chili powder for the salt rim.

¼ cup kosher salt, for rimming glasses

Lime wedge, for rimming glasses

4 ounces white tequila

2 ounces triple sec

1½ ounces freshly squeezed lime juice (from 2 limes)

Ice

Lime slices, for garnish

1. Place salt on a small shallow plate. Rim 2 glasses with a lime wedge, then dip in salt to coat rim.

2. Divide tequila, triple sec, and lime juice between 2 glasses and stir to combine. Top with ice and garnish with lime before serving.

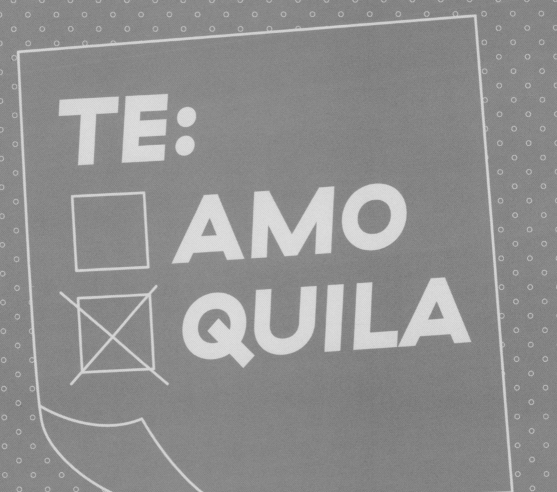

MAKE 'EM MINI!
Empty 5 (50–milliliter) chilled
Silver Patrón nips into a pitcher.
Add 4 ounces **triple sec** and
3 ounces freshly squeezed **lime
juice** and stir to combine.
Rim nips with **lime wedge**
and dip in **kosher salt** then fill
with **margarita mixture**.

STRAWBERRY JALAPEÑO MINT JULEP

SERVES 1 | TOTAL TIME: 45 MIN

Don't let Derby Day be your only excuse to make these juleps—they're worthy all year. If you're into spicy margs, then you'll be able to handle the heat here: The jalapeño-infused simple syrup mellows out once it hits the cool mint and sweet berries.

½ cup water

½ cup granulated sugar

2 jalapeños, halved

¼ cup chopped strawberries

8 fresh mint leaves

2 ounces bourbon

Ice

1 (12-ounce) can seltzer

Strawberry, for garnish

Red jalapeño, sliced, for garnish

1. Make jalepeño simple syrup: In a small saucepan over medium heat, combine water, sugar, and jalapeños. Bring to a boil, then reduce heat and simmer 10 minutes. Remove from heat and let cool to room temperature. Discard jalapeños.

2. In a cocktail glass, muddle strawberries and mint. Add bourbon and 1 tablespoon jalepeño simple syrup, then fill with ice and top off with seltzer.

3. Garnish with mint, a strawberry, and red jalapeño slices.

BOTTOMLESS

BRUNCH

TOAST WITH THE MOST

FRENCH COFFEE

Your morning cup of joe, but make it fancy. We double down on coffee flavor with the addition of Kahlúa plus some Cointreau for a rich orange flavor. Fair warning: This might ruin normal coffee for you!

---

1 ounce Kahlúa

1 ounce Cointreau

1½ cups hot coffee

1 teaspoon sugar

Whipped cream

Chocolate shavings, for garnish

1. In a glass mug, whisk together Kahlua, Cointreau, and coffee. Stir in sugar.

2. Top with whipped cream and chocolate shavings.

BAILEYS COFFEE SLUSHIES

SERVES 4 | TOTAL TIME: 3 HR 15 MIN

The best of both worlds for the bruncher who double-fists booze and coffee. Cold-brew ice cubes ensure your drink won't get watered down.

---

3 cups cold-brew coffee, divided

½ cup milk

¼ cup Baileys Irish Cream

¼ cup vodka

Chocolate sauce, for garnish

Caramel sauce, for garnish

Whipped cream, for garnish

1. Fill an ice-cube tray with 2½ cups coffee. Freeze until solid, 3 hours.

2. In a blender, combine frozen coffee cubes with remaining ½ cup coffee, milk, Baileys, and vodka. Blend until smooth.

3. Drizzle chocolate and caramel sauces into each glass. Divide slushy evenly among glasses, then top with whipped cream, more caramel, and more chocolate. Serve with straws.

MICHELADA

SERVES 1 | TOTAL TIME: 10 MIN

Part Mexican beer, part Bloody Mary, this hot sauce—spiked favorite combines lime juice, plenty of spice, and our favorite secret ingredient: a savory dash of soy sauce.

---

1 teaspoon salt, for rimming glasses

1 teaspoon chili powder, for rimming glasses

Lime wedges, for rimming glass and garnish

2 ounces fresh lime juice

2 teaspoons hot sauce

Dash soy sauce

Ice

1 (12-ounce) bottle light Mexican beer (such as Modelo or Tecate)

1. On a shallow plate, combine salt and chili powder. Rim a large glass with a lime wedge and dip in chili salt to coat.

2. In a tall glass, combine lime juice, hot sauce, and soy sauce and stir to combine. Fill glass with ice, then top with beer and stir lightly.

3. Garnish with a lime wedge before serving.

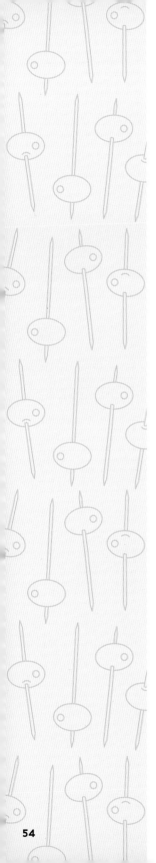

ULTIMATE BLOODY MARY

SERVES 4 | TOTAL TIME: 5 MIN

Everyone needs a Bloody in their brunch playbook—and everyone's got opinions on what makes the best one. To us, it's gotta be spicy and briny, with a sh*tload of black pepper. When we're really looking to Sunday Funday, we top 'em with mini grilled sandwiches or sliders.

4 cups tomato juice

1½ cups vodka

½ cup dill pickle juice

⅓ cup lemon juice

2 tablespoons prepared horseradish

1 tablespoon Worcestershire sauce

2 teaspoons hot sauce

½ teaspoon celery seeds

½ teaspoon freshly ground black pepper

Ice

Dill pickle spears, for garnish

Celery stalks, for garnish

Lemon wedges, for garnish

Olives, for garnish

1. In a large pitcher, combine tomato juice, vodka, pickle juice, lemon juice, horseradish, Worcestershire sauce, hot sauce, celery seeds, and black pepper.

2. Fill glasses with ice and top with Bloody Mary mixture. Garnish each with a dill pickle, celery stalk, lemon wedge, and olives.

**MAKE YOUR
BLOODY BRILLIANT**
Celery stalks and
pickle spears aren't the
only ways to garnish a
Bloody. We dreamed
up eight surprising
(and even more delish)
snacks to spike.

• Tater tots
• Shrimp
• Hard–boiled eggs
• Beef jerky
• Onion rings
• Bell pepper ring
• Cheddar cheese cube
• Pickled asparagus

TACO BLOODY MARIAS

SERVES 4 | TOTAL TIME: 40 MIN

A Bloody Maria is only as great as its garnish. And it really doesn't get any better than a mini taco.

8 small flour tortillas

1 tablespoon extra-virgin olive oil

½ lb. ground beef

½ teaspoon taco seasoning

Kosher salt

Freshly ground black pepper

3 cups tomato juice

1 cup white tequila

2 tablespoons Worcestershire sauce

1 tablespoon prepared horseradish

1 tablespoon hot sauce

Juice of ½ lime

Lime wedge, for rimming glasses

Ice

1. Make tacos: Use a 4-inch round cookie cutter to cut flour tortillas. Fold tortillas like tacos and place in toaster. Toast each tortilla until it holds its shape, 2 minutes.

2. In a medium skillet over medium heat, heat oil. Add ground beef and cook until no longer pink, 5 minutes. Add taco seasoning and season with salt and pepper. Divide beef among taco shells and top as desired.

3. Make Bloody Marias: In a large pitcher, combine tomato juice, tequila, Worcestershire, horseradish, hot sauce, lime juice, and pepper.

4. Rim 4 glasses with lime wedge. Place taco seasoning on a small plate and dip glasses in seasoning, turning to coat. Fill glasses with ice and pour in Bloody Maria mixture.

5. For each Bloody Mary, poke a wooden skewer through 2 tacos and place in drink, leaning tacos against rim.

FLAMIN' HOT BLOODY MARYS

SERVES 3 | TOTAL TIME: 15 MIN

Yeah, we went there. The cult Cheeto makes the most extreme Bloody Mary. We crush them up with lime zest for an electric rim, then top the drink with whole Cheetos for the photo op.

FOR THE RIM:

⅓ cup Flamin' Hot Cheetos, finely crushed

1 teaspoon lime zest

1 lime wedge

FOR THE BLOODY MARY:

2 cups tomato juice

1 cup vodka

2 tablespoons Worcestershire sauce

1 tablespoon horseradish

1 tablespoon hot sauce

Juice of ½ lime

Freshly ground black pepper

Ice

1. On a shallow plate, combine crushed Cheetos and lime zest. Rim glasses with a lime wedge and dip in crushed Cheetos.

2. In a large pitcher, stir together tomato juice, vodka, Worcestershire, horseradish, hot sauce, and lime juice, then season Bloody Mary mixture generously with pepper.

3. Add ice to glasses and fill with Bloody Mary mixture. Garnish each with a celery stalk, lime wedge, and a small handful of Cheetos. Serve with straws.

FOR TRUE CHEETOS LOVERS, a spicy rim is not enough! Top each drink with whole Cheetos for more crunch, and balance it out with a lime wedge and celery stick.

PICKLE BLOODY MARY SHOOTERS

SERVES 16 | TOTAL TIME: 20 MIN

Who doesn't love an edible shot glass? These shooters have everything we love: briny dill pickles, a savory Old Bay rim, and a boozy Bloody Mary mix with a dash of hot sauce. What's not to love?

---

8 large pickles

Old Bay seasoning, for rimming glasses

½ cup tomato juice, chilled

3 ounces vodka

½ tablespoon Worcestershire sauce

1 teaspoon horseradish

½ teaspoon hot sauce

Juice of ¼ lemon

Freshly ground black pepper

Celery leaves, for garnish

1. Make pickle shot glasses: Cut off the ends of each pickle so that both ends are flat, then cut each pickle in half crosswise. Using a quarter teaspoon, scoop out the middle of each pickle to create a well. Dip top of each pickle shot glass into Old Bay seasoning.

2. In a liquid measuring cup, combine tomato juice, vodka, Worcestershire, horseradish, hot sauce, lemon juice, and pepper. Stir until combined.

3. Pour into pickle shot glasses and garnish with celery leaves.

BRUNCH PUNCH

SERVES 10 | TOTAL TIME: 15 MIN

Truth: We'll never host brunch again without this. Spiked with vodka, it's essentially one giant mimosa boozy enough to hydrate your whole crew... and make everyone forget all about the bacon and eggs.

Ice

2 liters lemon–lime soda

1 (750–milliliter) bottle prosecco or champagne

2 cups orange juice

2 cups pineapple juice

2 cups vodka

2 cups sliced strawberries, plus more for rimming glasses

2 cups raspberries

1 cup fresh mint leaves, plus more for garnish

Sanding sugar, for rimming glasses

1. To a large punch bowl, add ice, soda, prosecco, orange juice, pineapple juice, vodka, strawberries, raspberries, and mint leaves and stir to combine.

2. Rim glasses with a fresh strawberry, then dip in sugar, turning to coat.

3. Ladle punch into glasses and garnish with more mint.

BOURBON MILK PUNCH

SERVES 4 | TOTAL TIME: 5 MIN

Tailgate like they do in the South with a batch of this creamy punch. It's basically a bourbon vanilla milkshake blended with honey and cinnamon. We're game.

Caramel sauce, for rimming glasses

2 tablespoons cinnamon sugar, for rimming glasses

1 (1.5–quart) container vanilla ice cream

1 cup bourbon

1 teaspoon pure vanilla extract

1 teaspoon honey

1 teaspoon ground cinnamon, plus more for garnish

Whipped cream, for garnish

1. Add caramel to one shallow dish and cinnamon sugar to another. Dip the rims of glasses in caramel then dip in cinnamon sugar, turning to coat.

2. In a blender, combine ice cream, bourbon, vanilla, honey, and cinnamon and blend until smooth.

3. Pour mixture into glasses and garnish with whipped cream and ground cinnamon.

TIFFANY MIMOSAS

SERVES 6 | TOTAL TIME: 5 MIN

The next best thing to treating yourself to some jewelry, these Tiffany–blue drinks get their classy color from blue curaçao, prosecco, and lemonade. Ribbon is optional, but it makes them extra sweet for shower season.

---

1 lemon wedge, for rimming glasses

2 tablespoons granulated sugar, for rimming glasses

1 ounce blue curaçao

1 (750–milliliter) bottle prosecco or champagne

2 cups lemonade

Thin white ribbon (optional)

1. Rim each champagne flute with lemon wedge, then dip in sugar.

2. Divide blue curaçao evenly among glasses. Fill halfway with bubbly, then top with lemonade.

3. If using ribbon, cut into 6–inch pieces and tie bows on stem of each glass.

RASPBERRY MIMOSA FLOATS

SERVES 4 | TOTAL TIME: 10 MIN

The only way to make a mimosa even better? Sorbet. Add the incredible duo of sparkling moscato and Chambord (the vanilla raspberry liqueur) to the mix and you're really good to go.

Lemon wedge, for rimming glasses

¼ cup granulated sugar, for rimming glasses

¼ cup raspberry sorbet

4 ounces Chambord

1 (750-milliliter) bottle sparkling moscato

Raspberries, for garnish

1. Rim champagne flutes with lemon wedge, then dip in sugar.

2. Place a small scoop of sorbet in each glass, then top with Chambord, sparkling moscato, and a few fresh raspberries.

APPLE CIDER MIMOSAS

SERVES 4 | TOTAL TIME: 3 HR 10 MIN

The first fall we dreamed these up, our fans went CRAZY—we hadn't realized the power of the mimosa. The magic of these: They feel special but are easy enough to eyeball. To a Delish staffer, cooking Thanksgiving dinner without one of these in your hand is a total crime.

2 tablespoons cinnamon sugar, for rimming glasses

1½ cups apple cider

1½ cups caramel vodka

1 (750–milliliter) bottle prosecco or champagne

Thinly sliced apples, for garnish

1. Dip champagne flutes in water to wet rims, then dip in cinnamon sugar.

2. Pour ¼ cup apple cider and ¼ cup caramel vodka into each flute and top off with bubbly. Garnish each flute with an apple slice.

CREAMSICLE MIMOSAS

SERVES 4 | TOTAL TIME: 5 MIN

Like Orange Julius's sophisticated older sister: The nostalgic combination of orange juice and heavy cream will bring you right back to your teenage mall rat days.

Orange slices, for rimming glasses and garnish

¼ cup granulated sugar, for rimming glasses

1 cup orange juice

1 tablespoon heavy cream

1 (750-milliliter) bottle prosecco or champagne

1. Rim champagne flutes with an orange wedge, then dip in sugar.

2. In a liquid-measuring cup, stir together orange juice and heavy cream until combined. Divide among champagne flutes and top off with bubbly.

3. Garnish each flute with an orange wedge.

GIRLS'

NIGHT
GRAB YOUR BOOZE CREWS

MOSCATO MARGARITAS

SERVES 4 | TOTAL TIME: 10 MIN

We're suckers for moscato. Here, the wine's floral, fruity notes find its soul mate with tequila and triple sec.

Lime wedges, for rimming glasses

¼ cup granulated sugar, for rimming glasses

1 cup chopped strawberries

1 cup white tequila

1 cup moscato

½ cup triple sec

½ cup lime juice

2 cups ice

1. Rim glasses with a lime wedge, then dip in sugar.

2. Combine strawberries, tequila, moscato, triple sec, lime juice, and ice in a blender. Blend until smooth, then divide mixture among 4 glasses.

3. Garnish with lime wedges before serving.

POUR IT UP, POUR IT UP

Moscato isn't the only wine that makes a killer marg. As long as you keep the ratio of 1 cup tequila to ½ cup triple sec to ½ cup lime juice, any type of wine will work.

**1½ cups rosé
+ 1 cup cubed watermelon
+ handful fresh mint**

————

**1 cup pinot noir
+ ½ cup grapefruit juice
+ grapefruit wedge**

————

**1½ cups prosecco
+ splash of orange juice
+ fresh thyme sprig**

CREAMSICLE PUNCH

SERVES 14 | TOTAL TIME: 10 MIN

Equal parts spectacle and crowd-pleaser. Vanilla ice cream delivers the creaminess, while prosecco and vodka, well, you know.

---

2 quarts orange juice

2 cups vodka

1 liter ginger ale

1 (750-milliliter) bottle prosecco

1 quart vanilla ice cream

1 orange, sliced into half-moons

1. In a large bowl, combine orange juice, vodka, ginger ale, and prosecco.

2. Carefully add scoops of vanilla ice cream and orange slices. Ladle into glasses and serve.

DON'T DO DAIRY? Orange sherbert works great as a replacement!

CHOCOLATE MARTINI

Bust out your favorite chick flick and shake up a batch of these 'tinis. Made with Baileys, vodka, and chocolate liqueur, this is essentially the naughty version of chocolate milk.

2 tablespoons chocolate syrup, plus more for drizzling

4 ounces Baileys Irish Cream

4 ounces chocolate liqueur

4 ounces vodka

Ice

Shaved chocolate for garnish

1. Pour chocolate syrup onto a shallow plate. Dip martini glasses into syrup to coat rims, then drizzle the inside of each glass with more chocolate syrup.

2. Combine Baileys, chocolate liqueur, and vodka in a large cocktail shaker. Fill with ice and shake until thoroughly chilled, 20 seconds. Divide evenly between glasses. Top with shaved chocolate, before serving.

COSMOS

Just because it was the drink of the '90s doesn't mean the cosmo isn't still one of our faves. Shake up lemon vodka, Cointreau, and cranberry and lime juices, and channel your inner Carrie Bradshaw.

Ice

4 ounces citrus vodka

2 ounces Cointreau

2 ounces cranberry juice

Juice of ½ lime

Lime wedge, for garnish

Cranberries, for garnish

1. Fill a cocktail shaker with ice and add vodka, Cointreau, cranberry juice, and lime juice.

2. Shake until well chilled. Strain into martini glasses and garnish with lime wedges and cranberries.

I save my carbs for wine. It's called PRIORITIES.

PINK SEÑORITAS

Like a margarita with a softer,
cuter side, the Señorita ditches limes for
pink lemonade and lemon juice.

**Lemon wedge, for
rimming glasses**

**Coarse salt, for
rimming glasses**

Ice

**2 ¼ cups pink
lemonade**

1 cup white tequila

¼ cup fresh lemon juice

¼ cup triple sec

**4 lemon slices,
for garnish**

Fresh mint, for garnish

1. Rim glasses with lemon
wedge, then dip rims in
salt. Fill glasses with ice.

2. To a pitcher, add pink
lemonade, tequila, lemon
juice, and triple sec. Stir
to combine, then divide
among glasses.

3. Garnish each glass with
a lemon slice and mint
before serving.

RED WINE MILKSHAKES

SERVES 4 | TOTAL TIME: 5 MIN

We love using our favorite bottle of red to spike hot cocoa, floats—even milkshakes. Blend some Pinot or Lambrusco (our favorite) with some vanilla ice cream and vodka and thank us later.

---

1 (1.5-quart) vanilla ice cream

1 cup red wine

½ cup vodka

Whipped cream, for garnish

Maraschino cherries, for garnish

1. In a blender, blend ice cream, red wine, and vodka until smooth.

2. Divide among glasses and garnish with whipped cream and cherries.

8-(WO)MAN MILKSHAKE

FIDDLESTIX
LAS VEGAS, NV

They say everything's bigger in Texas, but "they" clearly haven't been to Las Vegas. The city is home to all kinds of behemoth burgers and food challenges, but few are quite as head-turning as Fiddlestix's 8 Man Milkshake.

It's the kind that puts a classic fishbowl to shame, combining 120 ounces of ice cream—roughly two half-gallon containers—with 24 ounces of alcohol. Forget trying to find a glass to hold it in; only a full-size trifle dish can contain it. You can choose from the shop's trio of shake flavors, including Strawberry Cheesecake and Oh Captain, My Captain (that last one's made with spiced rum, caramel, and Cap'n Crunch, FYI).

The joint's showstopper is the Peanut Butter Cup though. It blends vanilla ice cream, chocolate sauce, peanut butter, Reese's Pieces, and bourbon. The whole thing's topped with whipped cream, Oreos—as is or deep-fried, if you want to go all out—and handfuls of rainbow sprinkles.

Don't let the name fool you: The mega milkshake can satisfy a dozen people... or just a few brave diners. (It has been done before.) It's Las Vegas at its most indulgent, perfect for bachelor and bachelorette parties where guests want to end the night on a sugar high. If there's any time to heed the call to go big or go home, Vegas is the place to do it.

DRUNKEN PB CUPS

A martini only a true Reese's Pieces fan can appreciate. To get the pure peanut butter flavor, we infuse vodka overnight with the candies. Chocolate syrup and peanut butter turn it into even more of a dessert.

FOR THE REESE'S–INFUSED VODKA:

1 cup vodka

½ cup Reese's Pieces

FOR THE COCKTAIL:

Ice

3 ounces Reese's–infused vodka

3 ounces milk

2 ounces chocolate liqueur

¼ cup peanut butter, for rimming glasses

½ cup crushed Reese's Pieces, for rimming glasses

2 Reese's peanut butter cups, for garnish

2 tablespoons chocolate syrup

1. Make Reese's–infused vodka: In a mason jar, combine vodka and Reese's pieces. Cover with tight–fitting lid and shake. Refrigerate overnight, then strain.

2. Make cocktail: Fill a cocktail shaker with ice, then pour in strained vodka, milk, and chocolate liqueur. Shake until chilled.

3. Rim glasses with peanut butter then dip in Reese's Pieces. Drizzle chocolate syrup into each glass then pour drinks and garnish with peanut butter cups.

TIRAMISU SHOTS

Our favorite Italian dessert in a glass? Yes, please. It takes a delicate pour to create perfect layers, but regardless of your finesse, the trifecta of Kahlúa, Baileys, and whipped cream tastes just like the real thing.

2 ounces Kahlúa

2 ounces Baileys

2 ounces heavy cream

Whipped cream, for garnish

Cocoa powder, for garnish

1. Divide Kahlúa among 4 shot glasses. Combine Baileys and heavy cream in a cocktail shaker, then slowly pour over Kahlúa.

2. Top with whipped cream and sprinkle with cocoa powder.

To achieve the **IMPRESSIVE LAYERS** choose a tall 2–ounce shot glass for serving.

BOOZY S'MORES SHAKES

SERVES 2 | TOTAL TIME: 10 MIN

We're constantly chasing the trifecta of gooey marshmallow, chocolate, and graham crackers.

8 large scoops chocolate ice cream

¼ cup Baileys Irish Cream

2 tablespoons vanilla vodka

½ cup marshmallow fluff

Crushed graham crackers, for rimming glasses

Marshmallow bits, for rimming glasses

Chocolate fudge, for rimming glasses

Whipped cream, for garnish

Chocolate squares, for garnish

Graham cracker squares, for garnish

1. In a blender, blend together ice cream, Baileys, vanilla vodka, and marshmallow fluff.

2. Combine crushed graham cracker and marshmallow bits on a small plate. Rim 2 glasses with chocolate fudge then dip in graham crackers and marshmallows.

3. Pour milkshake into glasses and top each shake with whipped cream, a chocolate square, and a graham cracker square.

YOU CAN SPIKE
THESE CHOCOLATE
MILKSHAKES
HOWEVER YOU
WANT...
We just recommend
sticking with the
mini marshmallow rim
for the look.

EXTRA

VIRGIN

MOCKTAILS FOR ANY OCCASION

BLACKBERRY FAUX-JITO

SERVES 4 | TOTAL TIME: 40 MIN

When you need to cool down during the summer, this spritzer is for you. We make it a little special with a mint simple syrup, which will impress even your bougiest of friends.

FOR THE MINT SIMPLE SYRUP:

½ cup packed fresh mint leaves, plus more for garnish

1 cup granulated sugar

1 cup water

FOR THE MOJITOS:

1 cup blackberries

1 teaspoon granulated sugar

½ cup lime juice

Ice

2 (12-ounce) cans seltzer

Mint, for garnish

1. Make mint simple syrup: In a small pot using a wooden spoon, crush mint leaves. Add sugar and water and bring to a boil over medium heat, stirring to dissolve sugar. Boil 3 minutes. Let cool, then strain out mint leaves, pressing with a wooden spoon to help release all liquid.

2. Make mojitos: In a small bowl, combine blackberries and sugar and use a wooden spoon to crush blackberries.

3. Divide mixture among glasses and add 2 tablespoons simple syrup and lime juice to each glass. Fill glasses with ice, then top off with seltzer and garnish with mint.

STIR IN any leftover simple syrup to lemonade, iced tea, or seltzer.

CRANBERRY BASIL *SANSGRIA*

SERVES 4 | TOTAL TIME: 10 MIN

Sangria sans the wine? Yes, please. The fruit is the real star here—use whatever's in season and get creative with the combination (think cranberries, orange slices, and rosemary for the holidays and mixed berries and mint for summer).

3 cups cranberry juice

Juice of 1 orange

1 (12-ounce) can seltzer

2 tablespoons honey

1 orange, sliced

1 apple, cored and sliced

⅓ cup frozen cranberries

¼ cup packed basil leaves

Ice

1. In a large pitcher, combine cranberry juice, orange juice, seltzer, and honey. Add fruit and basil and stir to combine.

2. Pour over ice to serve.

VIRGIN PIÑA COLADA

SERVES 2 | TOTAL TIME: 15 MIN

Raise your hand if this was the first "cocktail" you ever tasted. Even as an adult, these still taste like a milkshake. Highly recommend blending up a batch for the kids—and spiking yours.

1 (10-ounce) bag frozen pineapple chunks

4 large scoops vanilla ice cream

1 cup coconut milk

¾ cup pineapple juice

Pineapple wedge, for garnish

Maraschino cherry, for garnish

1. In a blender, blend together frozen pineapple, ice cream, coconut milk, and pineapple juice.

2. Divide between glasses and garnish with a pineapple wedge and a maraschino cherry.

APPLE CIDER SLUSHIES

SERVES 2 | TOTAL TIME: 5 MIN

If you've ever made a granita, you know
the drill for these: Freeze apple cider, lemon juice,
and cinnamon in a loaf pan for an hour, use a
fork to scrape (warning: this is oddly satisfying),
repeat until you have an icy slush. Cue the cuteness
overload with the mini apple–cider doughnut.

3 cups apple cider

1 lemon, juiced

**½ teaspoon
ground cinnamon**

**2 mini cinnamon-
sugar doughnuts
for garnish**

1. Pour cider, lemon juice, and
cinnamon in a loaf pan, whisking to
combine. Freeze for 1 hour.

2. Remove cider mixture from the freezer
and use a fork to scrape the slushy
mixture so it doesn't turn into a giant
ice cube. Once fully scraped and stirred,
return it to the freezer for 1 more hour.

3. Remove cider mixture from the
freezer once again, using a fork to
scrape and stir it into the consistency
of shaved ice. (If it's not frozen enough,
pop it back in the freezer for another
45 minutes.) Divide between glasses and
garnish each rim with a mini doughnut.

BEST-EVER ARNOLD PALMER

SERVES 8 | TOTAL TIME: 1 HR

During the dog days of August, we only crave this lemonade/iced tea thirst quencher. If you've never made lemonade from scratch before, now's the time— the freshly squeezed flavor is a game changer.

FOR THE LEMONADE:

3 cups water, divided

¾ cup granulated sugar

Juice of 6 large lemons (about ¾ cup)

FOR THE TEA:

4 cups water

⅓ cup honey

5 bags black tea

Ice

Fresh mint, for garnish

Lemon wedges, for garnish

1. Make lemonade: In a small pot over medium heat, bring 1 cup water and sugar to a boil, stirring to dissolve sugar. Boil 2 minutes. Let cool. Combine simple syrup, remaining 2 cups water, and lemon juice.

2. Make tea: In a medium pot over medium-high heat, bring water to a boil. Add honey and stir to dissolve. Turn off heat and add tea bags. Let steep 5 minutes. Let cool to room temperature.

3. In a large pitcher, combine lemonade and tea. Pour into glasses over ice and garnish with mint and lemon wedges.

ULTIMATE SHIRLEY TEMPLE

SERVES 4 | TOTAL TIME: 5 MIN

According to lore, the Shirley Temple was created for its namesake at Chasen's, a restaurant in Beverly Hills. We keep ours pretty classic, then spike it with fresh lime juice to cut through the sweetness.

Ice

3 cups lemon-lime soda

Juice of 1 lime

⅔ ounce grenadine

Lime wedges, for serving

Maraschino cherries, for serving

1. Fill glasses with ice. Divide soda and lime juice among glasses and top off with grenadine.

2. Garnish with a lime wedge and a maraschino cherry.

TRIPLE BERRY SPARKLERS

SERVES 6 | TOTAL TIME: 4 HR 15 MIN

Words of 4th of July wisdom: Don't get tanked if you're planning on playing with fire(works). When we need something that will keep the whole fam—from the kids to the grandparents—hydrated, this super-light, patriotic refresher is it.

FOR THE BERRY ICE CUBES:

1¼ cups coconut water

⅓ cup blueberries

⅓ cup raspberries

⅓ cup chopped strawberries

FOR THE DRINK:

2 tablespoons honey

2 tablespoons lime juice

2 tablespoons lemon juice

3 (12-ounce) cans seltzer

1. Make berry ice cubes: Place blueberries, raspberries, and strawberries in ice tray, then fill with coconut water. Freeze until frozen solid, 4 hours.

2. Make drink: In a pitcher or large measuring cup, combine honey with lime and lemon juices. Stir until honey is completely dissolved. Add seltzer and stir gently to combine.

3. Fill serving glasses with ice, then fill with lemon-lime mixture.

RASPBERRY MANGO MARGARITA SLUSHIES

SERVES 2 | TOTAL TIME: 20 MIN

When it's a real scorcher, refresh with these gorgeous frozen margs, made zesty with lots of lime. We love layering raspberry and mango for the sweet–tart tropical flavor, but strawberry and pineapple is a solid combo too.

FOR THE MANGO LAYER:

2 cups frozen mango

¾ cup coconut water

¼ cup lime juice

2 teaspoons honey

FOR THE RASPBERRY LAYER:

2 cups frozen raspberries

¾ cup coconut water

¼ cup lime juice

2 teaspoons honey

1. Make mango layer: Combine frozen mango, coconut water, lime juice, and honey in a blender. Blend until smooth, then fill each glass halfway full.

2. Make raspberry layer: Combine frozen raspberries, coconut water, lime juice, and honey in a blender. Blend until smooth, then top off each glass with mixture.

3. Garnish with lime wedges and serve.

BOOZY

BITES

JELL-O SHOTS AND MORE

NEGRONI JELL-O SHOTS

SERVES 18 | TOTAL TIME: 3 HR 30 MIN

Meghan Markle loves negronis, so we love negronis. Our obsession with the royals inspired these stunners. They're basically the classiest Jell-O shots ever. Period.

3 cups lemon-lime soda

4 (.25-ounce) packets unflavored gelatin

¼ cup granulated sugar

¼ cup gin

¼ cup Campari

¼ cup vermouth

¼ cup orange juice

Cooking spray, for pan

Sanding sugar, for garnish

Orange zest, for garnish

1. In a small saucepan, pour lemon-lime soda and sprinkle with gelatin. Let bloom, 2 minutes. Turn heat to medium and whisk until gelatin is dissolved. Remove from heat and stir in sugar, Campari, gin, vermouth, and orange juice.

2. Lightly grease a 9x5-inch loaf pan with cooking spray and pour in gelatin mixture. Chill until firm, about 3 hours.

3. Turn out gelatin mixture onto a piece of parchment paper and cover with sugar.

4. Garnish with orange zest then slice into squares.

CHOCOLATE STRAWBERRY JELL-O SHOTS

SERVES 25 | TOTAL TIME: 4 HR 25 MIN

A box of chocolates might be the way to someone's heart, but we'd rather a tray of these shooters with our ladies any day. Literally the perfect thing for a viewing party of *The Bachelorette* or Galentine's Day.

2 (16-ounce) containers strawberries

2 cups semisweet chocolate chips

2 teaspoons coconut oil

1 (3-ounce) box strawberry Jell-O

1 cup boiling water

1 cup vodka

1. Make shot glasses: Slice off tops and tips of strawberries, leveling them so they can stand up on a flat surface. Using a small melon baller, gently scoop out the inside of each strawberry to create a shot glass. Discard insides.

2. Line a baking sheet with parchment paper. Combine chocolate chips and coconut oil in a large bowl and microwave in 30-second intervals, stirring in between, until completely melted. Dip the bottoms of the hollowed-out strawberries in chocolate and place, open side up, on baking sheet. Refrigerate to harden, 10 minutes.

3. Meanwhile, make Jell-O filling: In a large bowl, whisk together Jell-O and boiling water until completely dissolved. Add vodka and whisk to combine.

4. Carefully pour Jell-O mixture into strawberries. Refrigerate until firm, 3 to 4 hours.

FIREBALL APPLE JELL-O SHOTS

SERVES 16 | TOTAL TIME: 4 HR 30 MIN

We did a bad, bad thing—but Fireball brings out, well, our fiery side. Using an apple as the vessel of a Jell-O shot is one of our favorite hacks. Pro tip: Don't skip the lemon juice. No one wants a brown apple.

---

6 apples, halved lengthwise, stems removed

Juice of 1 lemon

1 cup water

1 (3-ounce) packet cherry Jell-O

½ cup lemon-lime soda, chilled

½ cup Fireball whisky, chilled

1. Use a melon baller or teaspoon to hollow out apples, leaving a ¼-inch border. Brush cut surfaces with lemon juice. Place each apple hollow-side up in a muffin tin.

2. In a small saucepan, bring water to a boil, then pour into a heatproof bowl (or large liquid-measuring cup). Stir in Jell-O packet until completely dissolved. Whisk in soda and Fireball.

3. Carefully pour mixture into hollowed-out apples.

4. Refrigerate until firm, at least 4 hours.

5. Slice each apple half into 4 wedges before serving.

SOUR PATCH JELL-O SHOTS

SERVES 50 | TOTAL TIME: 2 HR 45 MIN

Sour Patch Kids are arguably our favorite sour candy; we can't see a movie without a pack. Choose a rainbow of Jell-O flavors to match the Kids. The shots themselves aren't sour—just the candy garnish.

1 (14-ounce) bag Sour Patch Kids, divided

5 cups boiling water, divided

1 (3.4-ounce) package strawberry Jell-O

1 (3.4-ounce) package orange Jell-O

1 (3.4-ounce) package lime Jell-O

1 (3.4-ounce) package berry blue Jell-O

1 (3.4-ounce) package lemon Jell-O

5 cups vodka, divided

Cool Whip, for garnish

Red, orange, green, blue, and yellow sanding sugar

1. Place a few Sour Patch Kids of each color at the bottom of 50 plastic shot glasses.

2. Pour 1 cup boiling water into a measuring cup and stir in strawberry Jell-O to dissolve. Whisk in 1 cup vodka. Pour mixture into the shot glasses that have the red Sour Patch Kids. Repeat with remaining boiling water, Jell-O flavors, vodka, and Sour Patch Kid colors.

3. Refrigerate until set, 2 hours.

4. Top each with Cool Whip, a Sour Patch Kid, and sanding sugar before serving.

PB&J JELL-O SHOTS

SERVES 18 | TOTAL TIME: 2 HR 15 MIN

These taste—and look—eerily similar to
the sandwich you binged as a kid. Getting flawless
layers is easier than you think: You just need to
let each one set 30 minutes before adding the next.

**FOR THE PEANUT
BUTTER LAYERS:**

1 cup water

**2 (.25-ounce) envelopes
unflavored gelatin**

**¾ cup smooth peanut
butter**

**2 tablespoons heavy
cream**

1 cup vodka

FOR THE JELLY LAYER:

½ cup water

**2 (.25-ounce) envelopes
unflavored gelatin**

½ grape jelly

½ cup vodka

Cooking spray

1. Make peanut butter mixture: In a small
saucepan, add water and sprinkle over
gelatin. Let bloom 2 minutes. Turn heat to
medium and whisk until gelatin is dissolved.
Remove from heat and whisk in peanut butter
and heavy cream until dissolved. Stir in vodka.
Pour into measuring cup and set aside.

2. Make jelly mixture: As in step 1, bloom and
dissolve gelatin. Then reduce heat to low and
whisk in jelly until dissolved. Remove from
heat and stir in vodka. Skim foam from top.

3. Grease a loaf pan with cooking spray and
add half the peanut butter mixture (about
1⅓ cup). Refrigerate 30 minutes or until
slightly firm. Add the jelly mixture and place
back in the refrigerator, 30 minutes more.
Add remaining peanut butter mixture,
then place in the refrigerator to firm up
completely, 1 to 2 hours more. Turn out onto
a cutting board, cut into squares, and serve.

Giving us major **B-J-E** (Big Jell-O Energy)

WHAT-A-MELON

Wait! Before you toss the scooped-out watermelon pulp, here's how we suggest you use it:

SALSA
Dice it up with chopped cucumber, jalapeño, red onion, mint, and lime juice.

GAZPACHO
Blend it with tomato, olive oil, jalapeño, and basil.

SALAD
Toss it with crumbled feta, chopped cilantro, and red onion.

BRUSCHETTA
Mix it up with basil, balsamic vinegar, honey, and crushed red chili flakes and spread it on grilled bread.

SUMMER SHANDY
Blend it up, then stir together with lemonade and top off with beer.

GIANT WATERMELON JELL-O SHOT

SERVES 8 | TOTAL TIME: 4 HR 20 MIN

With some careful pouring, turning a hollowed-out watermelon into a gelatinous party vessel is almost too easy. Serve slices on a platter and your friends are in for a jumbo surprise.

1 large watermelon

4 (3-ounce) boxes watermelon Jell-O

2 (1-ounce) boxes unflavored gelatin

4 cups boiling water

4 cups vodka

1. Halve watermelon and scoop out flesh. (Save for another use! See ideas at left.)

2. In a large mixing bowl, combine Jell-O mix and unflavored gelatin. Pour in boiling water and whisk until dissolved, 3 minutes. Add vodka and whisk until combined.

3. Transfer mixture to a pourable container (such as a glass measuring cup) and pour into halved watermelons.

4. Carefully transfer to a baking dish or baking sheet (lay on paper towels if the watermelon halves seem wobbly).

5. Refrigerate until firm, 4 to 5 hours.

6. Using a sharp knife, slice and serve immediately.

OREO JELL-O SHOT

SERVES 15 | TOTAL TIME: 5 HR 20 MIN

Even after a double take, you STILL won't believe these aren't the real thing. We kept the cookies but swapped the filling for a creamy vodka–spiked sweetened condensed milk center that will undoubtedly trick all of your friends.

Cooking spray

1 cup vodka

2 (.25-ounce) envelopes gelatin

1 cup boiling water

1 (14-ounce) can sweetened condensed milk

1 package Oreos

1. Grease a small sheet pan with cooking spray. In a large bowl or measuring cup, combine vodka and gelatin and let sit 2 minutes. Add boiling water and stir until gelatin dissolves completely. Pour in sweetened condensed milk and whisk to combine.

2. Pour gelatin mixture into prepared pan and refrigerate until firm, 4 to 5 hours.

3. Meanwhile, remove cream from Oreos using a butter knife. When gelatin mixture is firm, use a small biscuit cutter to cut gelatin mixture into rounds. Place 1 round between 2 Oreo cookies and repeat until all gelatin rounds are used.

LONG ISLAND ICED TEA JELL-O SHOTS

SERVES 24 | TOTAL TIME: 1 HR 25 MIN

You might think that your days of ordering a Long Island iced tea were long gone, but these might change your mind. Yup, these shots are pretty much pure booze, just like their namesake.

---

6 lemons

1 (12-ounce) can Coca-Cola

1 (.25-ounce) package unflavored gelatin

2 ounces triple sec

1 ounce vodka

1 ounce white tequila

1 ounce gin

1 ounce white rum

1. Slice lemons in half lengthwise. Juice lemons until you get 2 tablespoons juice. Using a spoon, scoop out the pulp of all lemons, leaving the peel intact. Place on a rimmed baking sheet and set aside.

2. In a small saucepan over medium-low heat, bring soda to a boil. Remove from heat and sprinkle in gelatin, then whisk until completely dissolved.

3. Add lemon juice and remaining ingredients, whisking to combine; transfer to a large measuring cup. Pour mixture into hollowed-out lemons and refrigerate until set, 1 hour. Slice lemons in half again and serve.

If you're having trouble **HOLLOWING OUT THE LEMONS,** make a shallow cut to detach pith at both ends.

BANANA PUDDING SHOTS

SERVES 12 | TOTAL TIME: 20 MIN

Banana pudding is our spirit dessert at Delish, so finding a way to make it boozy was a real power move. Rum and bananas are a natural pairing, only made better with crushed Nilla Wafers.

2 (3.4–ounce) packages instant vanilla pudding

1¼ cups milk

¾ cup white rum

1 banana, chopped

¼ cup crushed Nilla Wafers, plus more for garnish

Cool Whip, for garnish

½ banana, sliced

1. In a large bowl, whisk together pudding mix, milk, and rum. Fold in chopped bananas.

2. Spoon or pour pudding mixture into shot glasses until half full. Add a layer of crushed Nilla Wafers in each shot glass. Top with remaining pudding.

3. Garnish each pudding shot with a dollop of Cool Whip, a sprinkle of Nilla Wafers, and a slice of banana.

PUMPKIN PIE PUDDING SHOTS

Heck, these taste so much like pumpkin pie, you might wonder if you even need the dessert at Thanksgiving. If Fireball's not your thing (who are you even?!), vodka or bourbon works.

2 (3.4-ounce) boxes instant vanilla pudding mix

¾ cup milk

½ cup Fireball whisky

¼ cup vodka

½ cup pumpkin puree

1 teaspoon pumpkin pie spice

Whipped topping, for garnish

Cinnamon, for garnish

3 cinnamon graham crackers broken into quarters, for garnish

1. In a large bowl, whisk together vanilla pudding, milk, Fireball, vodka, pumpkin puree, and pumpkin pie spice.

2. Spoon into shot glasses and refrigerate until set, 1 hour.

3. Top each shot with whipped topping, a sprinkle of cinnamon, and a graham cracker.

S'MORES PUDDING SHOTS

SERVES 15 | TOTAL TIME: 1 HR 20 MIN

Cocktail or dessert? After your first bite, you won't care. Grab a spoon—and ask yourself why you're not putting marshmallow vodka into everything.

1 (3.9-ounce) package instant chocolate pudding

¾ cup milk

¼ cup marshmallow vodka

1½ ounces Cool Whip

5 tablespoons graham cracker crumbs

Cooking spray

15 large marshmallows

1½ Hershey's chocolate bars, broken into rectangles

1. In a large bowl, whisk together chocolate pudding mix and milk. Add vodka and whisk until combined. Fold in Cool Whip.

2. Add 1 teaspoon graham cracker crumbs to the bottom of each shot glass. Spoon or pipe chocolate pudding mix into shot glasses and refrigerate until chilled and firm, at least 1 hour.

3. When set, preheat oven to broil. Spray a small baking sheet with cooking spray and arrange marshmallows standing up on the tray. Broil until marshmallows are golden, 1 to 2 minutes. Keep an eye—it goes fast!

4. Using a small metal spatula, top each shot glass with a marshmallow and piece of chocolate.

PIÑA COLADA TRUFFLES

If you thought drinking piña coladas was addictive, try tossing them back like dessert.

---

1 (14-ounce) package Golden Oreos

1 (8-ounce) block cream cheese, softened

½ cup crushed pineapple

1 tablespoon coconut rum

2 cups white chocolate chips

1 tablespoon coconut oil

Toasted shredded coconut

1. Use a food processor to crush Oreos into fine crumbs. Transfer cookie crumbs to a large bowl. Add cream cheese, crushed pineapple, and rum and stir until evenly combined.

2. Line a baking sheet with parchment paper. Using a small cookie scoop, form mixture into small balls. Place on prepared baking sheet and freeze until slightly hardened, about 30 minutes, then roll balls until smooth.

3. In a medium microwave-safe bowl, melt white chocolate chips and coconut oil together in 30-second intervals. Working one at a time, dip frozen balls in melted chocolate and return to baking sheet. Sprinkle with toasted coconut.

4. Refrigerate until chocolate is hardened, 15 minutes or until ready to serve.

BAILEYS TRUFFLES

SERVES 16 | TOTAL TIME: 1 HR 30 MIN

We're making a batch of these fudgy bites for every chocolate lover on our holiday list. The totally sinful truffle base—Baileys, chocolate chips, and some heavy cream—only takes a few minutes to whip up.

2 cups semisweet chocolate chips

3 tablespoons heavy cream

¼ cup Baileys Irish Cream

Pinch kosher salt

1½ cups white chocolate chips

2 teaspoons coconut oil

Cinnamon sugar, for sprinkling

1. Set up a double boiler by placing a medium heatproof bowl over a small pot of simmering water. Add chocolate chips and heavy cream and stir until melted.

2. Turn off heat and stir in Baileys and salt. Refrigerate until chocolate mixture is firm enough to roll into balls, 1 hour.

3. In a medium heatproof bowl, microwave white chocolate and coconut oil together, in 20-second intervals, stirring after each interval, until melted.

4. Using a small cookie scoop, roll chocolate into 1-inch balls, then place on a parchment-lined baking sheet. Using a fork, dip each truffle into white chocolate, turning to coat. Place back on baking sheet and sprinkle with cinnamon sugar. Refrigerate until chocolate is hardened, 30 minutes, or until ready to serve.

SUMMER

DAZE

SUN'S OUT, FUN'S OUT

Aloha, Beaches!

BLUE HAWAIIAN COOLERS

SERVES 3 | TOTAL TIME: 15 MIN

Get a taste of island life without leaving your house by blending up these frozen drinks. Cream of coconut ensures the slushy isn't too icy. If you want them even creamier, use a full half-cup.

½ cup white rum

½ cup blue curaçao

¼ cup coconut rum

¼ cup cream of coconut

¼ cup pineapple juice

4 cups ice

Fresh pineapple slices, for garnish

Maraschino cherries, for garnish

1. In a blender, combine all ingredients with ice and blend until smooth.

2. Pour into 4 hurricane or highball glasses and garnish with pineapple slices and cherries.

STRAWBERRY FROSÉ

SERVES 6 | TOTAL TIME: 20 MIN

Yes way, frosé. This is the quintessential summer slushy: bottle of rosé, vodka, and frozen strawberries blended up with lemon juice.

---

1 (750-milliliter) bottle rosé, chilled

4 cups chopped strawberries

¼ cup vodka

2 tablespoons fresh lemon juice

8 cups ice

1. In a blender, combine about half the bottle of rosé, 2 cups strawberries, half the vodka, and half the lemon juice. Add about 4 cups of ice and blend until slushy.

2. Repeat with remaining ingredients.

3. Garnish with fresh strawberries.

BOOZY CHERRY BOMBS

SERVES 25 | TOTAL TIME: 1 HR 45 MIN

Light up your 4th of July party more than fireworks ever could with these Fireball-soaked maraschinos. If you're not feeling Fireball, bourbon has strong 'Merica vibes too.

---

1 (10-ounce) jar maraschino cherries with stems, drained

⅓ cup Fireball whiskey

⅓ cup whipped cream-flavored vodka

1 cup white chocolate chips

1 (3.25-ounce) bottle blue sanding sugar

1. Soak cherries in Fireball and vodka for 1 hour in the refrigerator. Remove cherries and pat dry with a paper towel.

2. Heat chocolate chips in the microwave in 20-second intervals, stirring in between, until fully melted.

3. Dip each cherry two-thirds of the way into the melted white chocolate, twisting slightly to help the chocolate stick. Then dip each cherry in blue sanding sugar, coating it halfway up the white chocolate coating.

4. Refrigerate 20 minutes before serving.

GIANT WATERMELON MARGARITA

CANTINA ROOFTOP
NEW YORK, NY

Cantina Rooftop in New York City went ahead and created a massive watermelon margarita served INSIDE an actual watermelon. Why, you might ask? Because there's no one in the world who doesn't want that, Cantina Rooftop manager Luis Flores says. Seriously.

The Cantina crew came up with the idea for the Big Ass Watermelon Margarita in a meeting last year: "We wanted to give our customers another option to enjoy a drink among friends... but to make it more fun and more special. So that each time someone ordered [the drink], it'd attract attention from other customers who'd then want it at their table."

The IRL viral marketing strategy worked: Since its 2018 debut, the Big Ass Marg remains super popular, and people are continually amazed by the grandeur of the drink.

In order to make this thing, an entire watermelon is cored and scooped. All the contents are puréed before being poured back inside the shell of the fruit with tequila, simple syrup, and enough lemon juice to counteract the sweetness of it all.

The margarita serves six to eight people, and comes in at $80, which is, quite honestly, a steal. Although the drink seems like the centerpiece of a summertime rooftop party, a marg big enough to keep a whole crew happy is good any time of year.

So bring a friend, two friends, three friends—as many as seven friends!—and roll on up to Cantina Rooftop whenever the urge for a huge, gigantic, big freakin' ass margarita strikes.

ULTIMATE HURRICANE

SERVES 2 | TOTAL TIME: 5 MIN

Invented in the Big Easy, this iconic cocktail is kinda like a daiquiri, only with passion fruit juice and grenadine. Serve it in a hurricane glass if you have one, but a stemless wine glass works just as well.

2 ounces white rum

3 ounces dark rum

6 ounces passion fruit juice

6 ounces orange juice

2 tablespoons grenadine

Ice

2 orange slices

2 maraschino cherries

1. In a large liquid-measuring cup, mix light rum, dark rum, juices, and grenadine.

2. Fill glasses with ice then pour drinks.

3. Garnish each glass with an orange slice and a maraschino cherry.

MOSCOW MULE PUNCH

SERVES 8 | TOTAL TIME: 10 MIN

You don't want to play bartender all night. This punch takes 10 minutes to stir together. Fresh mint isn't classic in a mule, but it adds dimension here.

4 cups ice

4 cups ginger beer

3 cups vodka

1 cup freshly squeezed lime juice

1 cup mint leaves, plus more for garnish

2 limes, sliced, plus more for garnish

1. In a large punch bowl, combine ice, ginger beer, vodka, lime juice, lime slices, and mint.

2. Ladle punch into glasses or copper mugs and garnish with more mint and lime slices.

DRINKING SOLO?
Fill a copper mug with **ice** then add 1 ounce **vodka** and ½ ounce **lime juice**. Top off with **ginger beer** and stir.

DOLE WHIP MARGARITAS

We're so obsessed with the Disney pineapple soft serve that we're always looking for an even more magical way to eat it. Part marg, part piña, these are dangerously addictive.

**Lime wedge,
for rimming glasses**

**Tajín or chili powder,
for rimming glasses**

4 cups frozen pineapple

½ cup white tequila

½ cup coconut milk

¼ cup fresh lime juice

**2 tablespoons
granulated sugar**

**Pineapple wedges,
for garnish**

1. Rim glasses with lime wedge and dip in Tajín.

2. Add frozen pineapple, tequila, coconut milk, lime juice, and sugar into blender and blend until smooth.

3. Pour into glasses or place mixture into a pastry bag fitted with a ¾-inch tip and swirl margarita into glass like frozen yogurt. Garnish each with a pineapple wedge.

COOK BLUEBERRIES in some water, sugar, and lemon juice until they burst—the leftover juice is what you're after. Use it here, then the leftovers in seltzer, vanilla ice cream, even yogurt.

BLUEBERRY LEMONADE MARGARITAS

SERVES 4 | TOTAL TIME: 25 MIN

The secret in these margs?
Blueberry simple syrup, which will make
you feel like a bona fide mixologist.

FOR THE BLUEBERRY SYRUP:

¼ cup granulated sugar

¼ cup water

½ cup blueberries

Zest of ½ lime

FOR THE MARGARITA:

2 tablespoons kosher salt,
for rimming glasses

2 tablespoons
granulated sugar, for
rimming glasses

1 lemon, cut into wedges

1 cup tequila

½ cup triple sec

1 cup lemonade

Ice

1. Make blueberry syrup: In a medium saucepan over medium heat, combine sugar and water and stir until sugar has dissolved. Add blueberries and lime zest and bring mixture to a boil. Reduce heat and simmer until blueberries have burst, about 5 minutes.

2. Remove from heat and let cool 10 minutes, then strain mixture into a clean jar. Let cool completely.

3. Make margarita: On a small plate, stir together sugar and salt. Rim each glass with a lemon wedge, then dip in sugar salt mixture. Divide tequila, triple sec, and lemonade among glasses. Fill each glass with ice, then top with blueberry syrup. Garnish with a lemon wedge and more blueberries.

SPARKLING TEQUILA SUNRISE

SERVES 1 | TOTAL TIME: 5 MIN

We're of the opinion that everything is better topped with bubbly, and this tequila sunrise is no different. Look for a drier champagne or prosecco—it'll help combat the sweetness of the pineapple juice.

Ice

4 ounces pineapple juice

1 ounce white tequila

½ ounce grenadine

Champagne or prosecco

1 orange peel

1 maraschino cherry

1 orange slice

1. Fill a tall glass with ice, then add pineapple juice and tequila. Add grenadine and top with champagne.

2. Roll orange peel against surface until twisted.

3. Garnish drink with orange peel twist, cherry, and orange slice.

SUMMER SHANDY PUNCH

SERVES 4 | TOTAL TIME: 2 HR 15 MIN

For the real dog days when you need to cool down with some fizz. Lemonade, ginger beer, and light wheat beer make a killer combination. We love adding citrus, but the other fruit is totally your call.

---

2 lemons, thinly sliced

2 limes, thinly sliced

1 apple, sliced

1 cup blueberries

1 (12-ounce) can ginger beer

2 (12-ounce) bottles wheat beer (such as Hoegaarden)

1 cups lemonade

½ cup seltzer

1. Combine all ingredients in a large pitcher (or a large bowl) and stir.

2. Chill for 2 hours or until cold.

PROSECCO PUNCH

SERVES 10 | TOTAL TIME: 15 MIN

Whether you're hosting book club, a pool party, or a cookie swap, this punch is here for you. Pineapple juice and vanilla vodka make this a cooler screwdriver. Change out these fruits for your favorites or whatever's around.

3 cups pineapple juice

3 cups seltzer water

1 (750–milliliter) bottle prosecco

1 cup vanilla vodka

2 cups sliced pineapple

2 peaches, thinly sliced

¼ cup mint, plus more for garnish

3 cups ice

10 wedges pineapple, for garnish

½ cup granulated sugar, for rimming glasses

1. Combine all ingredients except pineapple wedges and sugar in a punch bowl. Stir to combine.

2. Rim glasses with a pineapple wedge. Dip rims in sugar, then fill glasses with punch and garnish with pineapple and a sprig of mint before serving.

MAGIC MARGARITAS

SERVES 4 | TOTAL TIME: 4 HR 30 MIN

Prepare to lose your mind: PURPLE CABBAGE is the secret ingredient in these psychedelic margaritas. You won't taste the vegetable at all, but maybe don't tell your friends until after their first sip.

2 cups sliced purple cabbage

4 cups boiling water

1 cup white tequila

½ cup triple sec

⅓ cup freshly squeezed lime juice

1 cup lemonade

4 lime wedges, for garnish

¼ cup kosher salt for rimming glass

1. Place cabbage in a large heatproof bowl. Pour boiling water over cabbage and let sit until water turns deep blue, 5 minutes. Strain out cabbage and let water cool.

2. When water is no longer hot, transfer to ice trays. Freeze until solid, 4 hours.

3. In a pitcher or measuring cup, stir together tequila, triple sec, lime juice, and lemonade. Rim glasses with a lime wedge and dip in salt.

4. Place purple ice cubes in glasses and divide margarita among them. Garnish with a lime wedge before serving.

RAINBOW POPSICLES

SERVES 8 | TOTAL TIME: 4 HR 20 MIN

These three-ingredient pops are nothing short of magical. They're just the right amount of boozy and insanely adorable, and they have a seriously sour kick from the candy belts. Downing five in one sitting is shockingly easy, but beware of the sugar crash.

2 cups lemon-lime soda

¼ cups vodka

16 Airheads Xtreme Sour Belts

1. In a large bowl or glass measuring cup, combine lemon-lime soda and vodka and stir to combine.

2. Wrap two sour belts around the inside of a Dixie cup, then divide vodka mixture among cups.

3. Cover each cup with a piece of foil and cut a small slit in middle of foil. Insert a wooden popsicle stick into slit.

4. Freeze until solid, at least 4 hours.

5. When ready to serve, cut open the Dixie cups and peel them away from the pops.

MOSCOW MULE POPS

SERVES 10 | TOTAL TIME: 5 HR 10 MIN

A party in a pop: Your squad will bow down for these limeade–vodka icy cocktails. Pro move: Freeze your serving tray so the pops keep their chill.

2 cups
ginger beer

1 cup limeade

½ cup vodka

2 limes, zested
and juiced

Popsicle sticks

Zest of 2 limes,
for garnish

2 tablespoons
sanding sugar,
for garnish

1. In a large bowl or glass measuring cup, combine ginger beer, limeade, vodka, lime juice, and lime zest. Whisk until combined.

2. Divide mixture among pop molds and insert a popsicle stick into the center of each.

3. Freeze until solid, at least 5 hours and up to overnight.

4. Mix zest of 2 limes with sanding sugar. When ready to serve, sprinkle pops with sugar mixture.

GIN & TONIC POPS

SERVES 12 | TOTAL TIME: 5 HR 15 MIN

A boozy pop is more essential to a summer get–together than sunscreen. (Okay, okay, but you get it.) When you make them in little paper cups, there's virtually no cleanup. Sweetened condensed milk ensures they stay creamy even when frozen.

---

1 (14–ounce) can sweetened condensed milk

1 cup limeade

1 cup tonic water

½ cup gin

Juice and zest of 1 lime

12 lime slices, ¼–inch thick

12 Dixie cups

12 popsicle sticks or wooden spoons

1. In a large bowl or liquid measuring cup, combine sweetened condensed milk, limeade, tonic, gin, lime juice, and lime zest. Whisk until combined. Divide mixture among 12 Dixie cups.

2. Push a popsicle stick through the center of a lime slice, then insert the stick into a cup, making sure there is no room between the mixture and the lime slice. Repeat for all cups.

3. Freeze until solid, at least 5 hours and up to overnight.

4. When ready to serve, cut open the Dixie cups and peel them away from the pops.

BLOODY MARY POPS

SERVES 10 | TOTAL TIME: 6 HR 15 MIN

When the kitchen thought to use a celery stalk as the popsicle stick for these, we got giddy. Tomato juice, vodka, Worcestershire, and pickle juice make up the Bloody base of these almost–too–adorable–to–handle pops.

2 cups tomato juice

¼ cup vodka

2 tablespoons Worcestershire sauce

1 tablespoon pickle juice

2 teaspoons hot sauce

Juice of 1 lime

10 celery sticks, cut 4–inches in length

Flaky sea salt, for garnish

Old Bay seasoning, for garnish

1. In a large liquid measuring cup, whisk together tomato juice, vodka, Worcestershire sauce, pickle juice, hot sauce, and lime juice.

2. Divide mixture among pop molds, then insert a celery stick into each pop.

3. Freeze until solid, 6 hours.

4. When ready to serve, sprinkle pops with flaky sea salt and Old Bay and serve immediately.

FALL

FORWARD

FIREPLACE RECOMMENDED

APPLE CIDER SANGRIA

SERVES 6 | TOTAL TIME: 10 MIN

Who says sangria's just for summer?
This white wine concoction is what we drink
every weekend during the transition from
summer to fall. Make it pretty by slicing a few
different types of apples.

1 Granny Smith apple, diced

1 Honeycrisp apple, diced

1 lemon, sliced

1 orange, sliced and quartered

2 cups apple cider, chilled

1 (12-ounce) can ginger beer, chilled

1 (750-milliliter) bottle white wine, chilled

1. Fill large pitcher with fruit, then add apple cider, ginger beer, and white wine.

2. Stir mixture and pour into serving glasses.

HARVEST PUNCH

PSA: Don't do any fall activity without this. We love the combo of apple cider and ginger beer, made even more fizzy with prosecco. Cinnamon sticks are not necessary, but bring more #FallVibes.

6 cups ice

½ gallon apple cider

1 (750–milliliter) bottle prosecco

1 cup vodka

2 (12–ounce) bottles ginger beer

3 apples, sliced

2 oranges, sliced

8 cinnamon sticks

Cinnamon sugar, for rimming glass

1. In a large punch bowl, add ice. Pour in apple cider, prosecco, vodka, and ginger beer. Add apples, oranges, and cinnamon sticks and stir to combine.

2. Rim glasses with an orange slice, then dip into cinnamon sugar, turning to coat. Serve punch in rimmed glasses.

MULLED WINE

The ultimate partner in cozy. You might think mulled anything takes forever to simmer—our version takes 10 minutes on the stove from start to finish.

---

1 (750-milliliter) bottle red wine

1 orange, sliced, plus more for garnish

6 whole cloves

3 cinnamon sticks

3 star anise

¼ cup honey

½ cup brandy

1. In a medium saucepan over medium heat, combine all ingredients. Bring to a simmer (not a boil), then reduce heat to medium-low. Simmer gently over low heat for 10 minutes.

2. Serve warm and garnish with orange.

MULLED OVER
Hosting a party? We love making a big batch of mulled wine in our slow cooker for friends. Add all the same ingredients plus 1 cup each apple cider and cranberry juice to stretch it for a crowd, cook on high for 30 minutes, and serve it up.

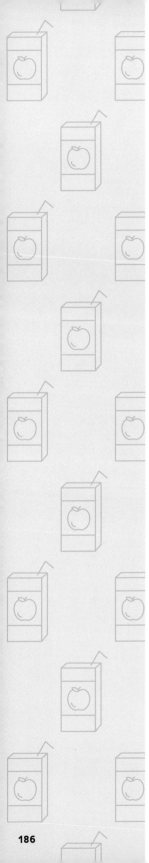

APPLE PIE MOONSHINE

SERVES 6 | TOTAL TIME: 1 HR 15 MIN

Prohibition might be over, but moonshine is still very much en vogue. It's not as illicit as it sounds: All you need is high-proof alcohol (like Everclear), vodka, and apple juice to make a batch at home.

4 cups apple juice

4 cups apple cider

¾ cup granulated sugar

¼ cup packed brown sugar

2 cinnamon sticks

½ teaspoon ground ginger

½ teaspoon ground allspice

¾ cup 190-proof grain alcohol

¾ cup vodka

1. In a large pot over medium-high heat, combine apple juice, cider, sugars, cinnamon sticks, and spices. Bring to a simmer, then cover pot with lid and reduce heat to medium-low.

2. Simmer for 1 hour, then remove from heat and let cool.

3. Remove cinnamon sticks and stir in grain alcohol and vodka. Transfer to jars or bottles.

4. Shake well before serving.

BUTTERBEER PUNCH

SERVES 9 | TOTAL TIME: 15 MIN

No matter what Hogwarts house you're in, we can all agree that this spiked butterbeer is legit. Cream soda is the key to recreating Harry's drink. We make it for grown-ups with vanilla vodka.

FOR THE WHIPPED TOPPING:

2 cups heavy cream

2 tablespoons brown sugar

1 teaspoon vanilla

2 tablespoons melted butter

FOR THE PUNCH:

6 (12-ounce) cans cream soda

3 (12-ounce) cans seltzer

3½ cups vanilla vodka

Gold sanding sugar, for garnish

Butterscotch syrup, for garnish

1. Make topping: In a large bowl, combine cream, brown sugar, and vanilla. Using a hand mixer, whip until soft peaks form. Fold in melted butter and set aside.

2. Make punch: In a punch bowl, combine cream soda, seltzer, and vodka. Top with whipped cream and a sprinkle of gold sanding sugar.

3. Drizzle butterscotch syrup on rim of mugs. Serve punch and top with additional sanding sugar and butterscotch syrup.

CARAMEL HOT TODDY

SERVES 3 | TOTAL TIME: 20 MIN

On a freezing day, nothing has the power to warm us up more than a hot toddy. The combination of hot water, lemon juice, and bourbon is as soothing as it is boozy. We make it even better by melting our favorite childhood candy, Werther's Caramels, into the mix.

10 Werther's Original Hard Candies, crushed

¼ cup caramel sauce

2 cups water

10 Werther's Original Hard Candies, whole

2 cinnamon sticks, plus more for serving

¼ cup whiskey or bourbon

⅓ cup lemon juice

Lemon slices, for serving

1. Place crushed Werther's on a shallow plate and caramel on a separate shallow plate. Dip rims first in caramel then in crushed Werther's.

2. In a small saucepan over medium heat, combine water, Werther's, and cinnamon sticks. Stir constantly until candies are fully melted. Turn off heat and stir whiskey (or bourbon) and lemon juice.

3. Ladle into mugs and serve with cinnamon sticks and lemon slices.

TOUCHDOWN PUNCH

SERVES 10 | TOTAL TIME: 10 MIN

When your tailgating crew is looking to get sloshed before halftime, this punch— a mixture of blue curaçao, vodka, and prosecco—will score you major points.

---

3 cups ice

1 liter lemon–lime soda (such as Sprite)

4 cups seltzer water

1 (750–milliliter) bottle prosecco

1 cup vodka

¼ cup blue curaçao

1 lemon, thinly sliced

1. In a punch bowl or large pitcher, add ice. Pour in soda, seltzer, prosecco, vodka, and blue curaçao.

2. Add lemon slices and stir to combine.

PECAN PIE MARTINIS

SERVES 3 | TOTAL TIME: 20 MIN

Strong enough to help you get through a Thanksgiving dinner with the craziest of uncles and in-laws. Rumchata, crème de cacao, and bourbon pose a delicious triple threat.

---

3 tablespoons caramel sauce, for rimming glasses

¼ cup toasted chopped pecans, for rimming glasses

⅔ cup rumchata

⅔ cup crème de cacao

⅓ cup bourbon

Ice

Cool Whip, for garnish

3 whole pecans, for garnish

Ground cinnamon, for garnish

1. Place caramel and toasted chopped pecans on separate small shallow plates. Dip the rim of each glass first into caramel and then into chopped pecans to coat.

2. Combine rumchata, crème de cacao, and bourbon in a large cocktail shaker. Fill with ice and shake until cold, 30 seconds. Pour into martini glasses and top with a dollop of Cool Whip, a whole pecan, and a sprinkle of cinnamon.

BLACK MAGIC MARGARITAS

Trick or tequila. The Sanderson sisters
would totally get down with these noir cocktails.
We're not usually fans of food coloring,
but when red, green, and blue combine, the
result is too spooky to resist.

Lime slices,
for garnish

2 tablespoons black
sanding sugar

4 ounces white
tequila

4 ounces lime juice

2 ounces triple sec

Red food coloring

Blue food coloring

Green food coloring

Ice

1. Rim 2 glasses with a lime slice
and dip in black sanding sugar.

2. Divide tequila, lime juice,
and triple sec between 2 glasses
and stir to combine. Add food
coloring until desired black color
is achieved.

3. Add ice and garnish with lime
slices before serving.

BOOZY SCREAMSICLES

SERVES 4 | TOTAL TIME: 10 MIN

Sip on one of these while you greet trick-or-treaters. Orange sherbet, vanilla vodka, and milk blended up tastes just like a creamsicle. Lining the inside of the milkshake glass with chocolate sauce will make it look legit.

Chocolate sauce, for garnish

12 Oreos, finely crushed

1 quart orange sherbet

1 cup vanilla vodka

¾ cup milk

Whipped cream, for garnish

Orange and black sprinkles, for garnish

1. Pour 2 tablespoons chocolate sauce onto a small plate. Place Oreo crumbs on a second small plate. Dip rims of serving glasses first in chocolate sauce, then in Oreo crumbs.

2. Combine sherbet, vodka, and milk in a blender and blend to combine. Drizzle some chocolate sauce on the inside of each serving glass, then fill with milkshake. Garnish with whipped cream, remaining Oreo crumbs, and sprinkles.

'TIS THE

SEASON

GET INTO THE HOLIDAY SPIRITS

As the name implies, this recipe does have eggs, but they're not raw. YOU TEMPER THEM which is just the scientific-sounding term for slowly streaming in hot liquid so the eggs don't scramble. Spiking with bourbon or rum are both traditional.

Save the neck for me, Clark!

ULTIMATE EGGNOG

SERVES 4 | TOTAL TIME: 1 HR 20 MIN

There are two types of people in this world: those who like eggnog and those who despise it. We fall into the camp that starts making 'nog right after Thanksgiving.

2 cups whole milk

½ teaspoon ground cinnamon, plus more for garnish

½ teaspoon ground nutmeg

½ teaspoon pure vanilla extract

6 large egg yolks

½ cup granulated sugar

1 cup heavy cream

1 cup bourbon or rum

Whipped cream, for serving

1. In a small saucepan over low heat, combine milk, cinnamon, nutmeg, and vanilla and slowly bring mixture to a low boil.

2. Meanwhile, in a large bowl, whisk egg yolks with sugar until yolks are pale in color. Slowly add hot milk mixture to egg yolks in batches to temper eggs and whisk until combined.

3. Return mixture to saucepan and cook over medium heat until slightly thick (and coats the back of a spoon) but does not boil. (If using a candy thermometer, mixture should reach 160°F.)

4. Remove from heat and stir in heavy cream and booze.

5. Refrigerate until chilled.

6. When ready to serve, garnish with whipped cream and cinnamon.

WHITE CHRISTMAS MARGARITAS

SERVES 6 | TOTAL TIME: 15 MIN

Dream hard enough for a white Christmas and you'll get one. These drinks are part margarita, part piña colada, thanks to a full can of coconut cream. Cranberries (fresh and frozen both work) add the festive decor.

1 (14-ounce) can unsweetened coconut milk

1½ cups silver tequila

1 cup triple sec

¼ cup lime juice

4 cups ice

1 lime, sliced for garnish

Lime wedges, for rimming glasses and garnish

Sanding sugar, for rimming glasses

Cranberries, for garnish

1. Combine coconut milk, tequila, triple sec, lime juice, and ice in a blender. Blend until smooth.

2. Rim glasses with a lime wedge and dip in sanding sugar. Pour mixture into glasses, and garnish with lime and cranberries.

CHRISTMOSAS

Open presents with your right hand, hold one of these in your left. Mix up the sparkling grape juice and prosecco base, then stir in whatever fruit looks festive, like cranberries, pomegranate seeds, and grapes.

2 Granny Smith apples, chopped

1 cup whole fresh cranberries

1 cup green grapes, halved

1 cup pomegranate seeds

1 cup sparkling grape juice, chilled

1 (750-milliliter) bottle champagne, prosecco, or cava, chilled

1. In a large pitcher or punch bowl, combine apples, cranberries, grapes, and pomegranate seeds.

2. Pour in sparkling grape juice and champagne, and stir to combine.

SLOW-COOKER RED WINE HOT COCOA

SERVES 6 | TOTAL TIME: 1 HR 5 MIN

When we brewed up the first batch of this, we were all skeptical—red wine and chocolate?! Made with a whole bottle, it's truly the best of both worlds.

2½ cups semi-sweet chocolate chips

¼ cup cocoa powder

½ cup granulated sugar

Pinch kosher salt

6 cups whole milk

1 (750-milliliter) bottle red wine

Cooking spray

Marshmallows, for garnish

Chocolate shavings, for garnish

1. Combine chocolate chips, cocoa powder, sugar, salt, milk, and wine in a slow cooker. Cook on high for 1 hour, whisking every 20 minutes.

2. Preheat oven to broil. Grease a small baking sheet with cooking spray and arrange marshmallows standing up on the tray. Broil until marshmallows are golden, 1 to 2 minutes.

3. Ladle cocoa into mugs and top with toasted marshmallows and chocolate shavings.

GRINCHY PUNCH

SERVES 8 | TOTAL TIME: 20 MIN

A punch that will make anyone's heart grow three sizes, Grinch or not. To get the glowing green look, lemon-lime Kool-Aid is your best bet. If you're serving kids, ditch the vodka.

1 (.17-oz) packet
Kool-Aid
lemon-lime mix

4 cups water

4 cups ice

3 cups lemon-lime soda

2 cups pineapple juice

2 cups vodka

1 cup ginger ale

Lime wedges, for
rimming glasses

Red sanding sugar, for
rimming glasses

1. In a large pitcher, combine Kool-Aid and water.

2. In a large punch bowl, combine ice, Kool-Aid, soda, pineapple juice, vodka, and ginger ale, and stir to combine.

3. Rim glasses with a lime wedge and dip in sanding sugar to coat. Pour punch into glasses to serve.

MISTLETOE MARGARITAS

SERVES 6 | TOTAL TIME: 20 MIN

Blend up a batch of these cranberry juice frozen margs before you meet anyone under the mistletoe. This recipe also works great for margaritas on the rocks.

½ cup whole cranberries

½ cup lime juice, divided

¼ cup granulated sugar, divided

2 tablespoons kosher salt, for rimming glasses

1 wedge lime, for rimming glasses

2 cups cranberry juice

1½ cups silver tequila

1 cup triple sec

12 cups ice

Mint, for garnish

1. In a medium bowl, toss cranberries with ¼ cup lime juice. Drain out lime juice, then toss with 2 tablespoons sugar. Pour onto a baking sheet to dry.

2. Combine remaining sugar with salt on a shallow plate and mix to combine. Rim each glass with a lime wedge, then dip in sugar–salt mixture.

3. Working in batches if necessary: Combine cranberry juice, tequila, triple sec, remaining ¼ cup lime juice, and ice in a large blender. Blend until smooth. Pour into prepared glasses and garnish with a sprig of mint and a couple of sugared cranberries.

MISTLETOE JELL-O SHOTS

SERVES 22 | TOTAL TIME: 1 HR 20 MIN

"Is it even a holiday party without Jell-O shots? Not in our book. We spike lime Jell-O with vodka, but silver tequila or gin also work here. Whipped cream, mint, and Red Hots make 'em really lit.

Lime wedge, for rimming glasses

Red sanding sugar, for rimming glasses

1 cup water

2 (3.4-ounce) packets lime Jell-O

1 cup vodka, chilled

Whipped cream, for garnish

Mint leaves, for garnish

Red Hots, for garnish

1. Rim each shot glass with lime wedge, then dip into sanding sugar.

2. Bring water to a boil in a medium saucepan. Once bubbling, add lime Jell-O mix, stirring until completely dissolved. Turn off heat. Stir in vodka. Transfer mixture to a liquid measuring cup or a small pitcher, then pour into each shot glass. Refrigerate glasses until Jell-O sets, 2 hours.

3. Garnish with whipped cream, mint leaves, and Red Hots before serving.

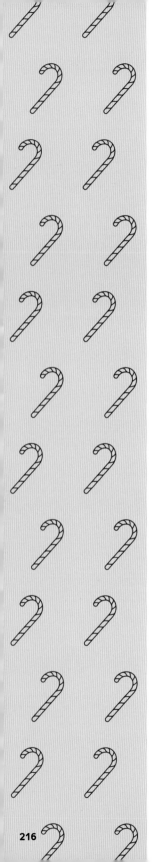

PEPPERMINT BARKMIMOSAS

SERVES 6 | TOTAL TIME: 10 MIN

Classy enough to serve at brunch, strong enough to light up your ugly-sweater party. The crushed candy cane—chocolate rim is Pinterest-y in the best way.

¼ cup semisweet chocolate chips, melted, for rimming glasses

3 candy canes, crushed, for rimming glasses

6 ounces peppermint schnapps, divided

1 (750-milliliter) bottle champagne or prosecco, chilled

6 candy canes, whole

1. Pour melted chocolate onto a small plate. Pour crushed candy canes onto a separate plate. Dip rims of champagne flutes first in chocolate, then in crushed candy canes to coat.

2. Add 1 ounce peppermint schnapps to each glass, then top with champagne or prosecco. Garnish with whole candy canes before serving.

HOT BUTTERED RUM

SERVES 4 | TOTAL TIME: 2 HR 20 MIN

If you're asking yourself, *What is hot buttered rum anyway?* you're not alone. It's essentially a batter of brown sugar and softened butter that you spike with rum. Our secret ingredient? Melted vanilla ice cream, which makes it super addictive.

FOR THE BUTTERED RUM BATTER:

4 tablespoons butter, softened

3 tablespoons packed brown sugar

½ cup vanilla ice cream, softened

½ teaspoon ground cinnamon

FOR THE RUM DRINK:

2 cups apple cider

1 cup rum

1. Make the buttered rum batter: In a mixing bowl, beat butter and brown sugar until light and fluffy. Beat in ice cream and cinnamon, then spoon mixture into a mason jar or resealable container. Store in freezer until mostly hardened, 2 hours or until ready to serve.

2. Make the drinks: In a medium saucepan, heat cider until boiling, stirring occasionally. Remove from heat and pour into a pitcher.

3. Place 2 tablespoons of buttered rum batter into each mug. Fill ⅓ full with rum, then top with hot apple cider. Stir before serving.

IT'S BEGINNING TO LOOK A LOT LIKE COCKTAILS

RUMCHATA HOT COCOA

We've been riding the RumChata train since day one, putting the creamy liqueur in eggnog, cupcakes, even cheesecake. Its cinnamon-laced flavor is the perfect match for super-rich and chocolaty cocoa.

2½ cups whole milk

¼ cup granulated sugar

2 tablespoons cocoa powder

1 cup chocolate chips

1 teaspoon pure vanilla extract

½ cup Rumchata

⅓ cup caramel sauce

Whipped cream, for garnish

Cinnamon sugar, for garnish

Cinnamon stick, for garnish

1. In a small saucepan over medium heat, bring milk to a simmer. Whisk in sugar and cocoa powder and stir until no lumps remain. Stir in chocolate chips and vanilla and cook, stirring occasionally, until chocolate is completely melted. Stir in Rumchata, then turn off heat.

2. Pour caramel into a small dish. Dip cups in caramel to coat rim. Pour hot chocolate into each glass, then top with whipped cream, a sprinkle of cinnamon sugar, more caramel, and a cinnamon stick.

DRUNK JACK FROSTIES

SERVES 4 | TOTAL TIME: 10 MIN

Book Jack Frost on the first plane to warmer temps with these blended drinks. They look wintry, but the combo of blue curacao, lemonade, vodka, and champagne tastes like summer.

1 cup vodka

1 cup champagne

½ cup blue curaçao

½ cup lemonade

6 cups ice

Lemon wedge, for rimming glasses

White sanding sugar, for rimming glasses

1. In a blender, combine vodka, champagne, blue curaçao, lemonade, and ice. Blend until combined.

2. Rim each glass with a lemon wedge, then dip in sanding sugar.

3. Pour frosties into rimmed glasses and serve immediately.

JINGLE JUICE

File this one under holiday survival guide. Your whole family will love the duo of cranapple juice and red moscato. Want a wine that's not as sweet? Sub in rosé or pinot.

Lime wedge, for rimming glasses

½ cup sugar, for rimming glasses

4 cups cranapple juice

2 (750-milliliter) bottles red moscato

1 (750-milliliter) bottle prosecco

½ cup vodka

2 cups frozen cranberries

⅓ cup mint leaves

2 limes, sliced into rounds

1. Rim glasses with a lime wedge, then dip in sugar until coated.

2. Combine all ingredients in a punch bowl, and stir until combined.

3. Chill if necessary before serving.

SUGAR COOKIE MARTINIS

SERVES 2 | TOTAL TIME: 45 MIN

Crank up Mariah Carey's Christmas album, pull a tray of cookies out of the oven, and sip on these while you decorate. The amaretto and Baileys combo is something you'll want to adopt all winter.

FOR THE RIM:

Refrigerated sugar cookie dough

½ cup vanilla frosting

¼ cup sprinkles, plus 1 teaspoon, divided

FOR THE MARTINI:

½ cup whole milk

¼ cup Baileys Irish Cream

¼ cup vanilla vodka

¼ cup amaretto

Ice

1. Preheat oven to 350°F and line a baking sheet with parchment paper. Roll sugar-cookie dough out to ¼-inch thick. Using a cookie cutter, cut out desired shapes, then place cookies on prepared baking sheet. Bake until just set and lightly golden around the edges, 12 minutes. Let cool.

2. Using an offset spatula, spread a thin layer of frosting onto rims of glasses. Pour ¼ cup sprinkles onto a small plate, then dip rims in sprinkles to coat. Use an offset spatula to frost cookies, then decorate with remaining 2 tablespoons sprinkles.

3. In a cocktail shaker, combine milk, Baileys, vodka, and amaretto. Add ice and shake until cold. Pour into glasses and garnish with a cookie.

CHEERS...

To the incredible Delish team, including **Lena Abraham**, **Lauren Miyashiro**, **Lindsey Ramsey**, **Lindsay Funston**, **Sarah Weinberg**, **Makinze Gore**, **June Xie**, **Tess Koman**, and **Julia Smith**; to our amazing art director **Allie Folino**, our cover star **Jessica Musumeci**, and our fantastic designer **Sabrina Contratti**; to our mentors at Hearst, including **Kate Lewis** and **Troy Young**; to our friends and partners at Hearst Books, including **Jacqueline Deval**, **Nicole Fisher**, **Nickolas Young**, **Kevin Jones**, and **Brian McCoach**; and to my family, **Scott**, **Spencer**, **Teddy**, and **Everett**, who make me feel like the luckiest person in the world and who never, ever drive me to drink.

CREDITS

Cover Photography
Chelsea Kyle

Cover Food Styling
Micah Morton

Cover Art Direction
Jessica Musumeci

Book Illustrations
Alexandra Folino

Interior Photography

Emily Hlaváč Green: 4–7, 10–12, 14–15, 17, 20–21, 23–27, 30–31, 33–35, 37, 39, 42–44, 46–48, 57, 66, 74–75, 82–83, 92–93, 96–97, 99, 101–102, 106–112, 114–115, 118, 120–122, 130–131, 135, 140, 142–149, 162–163, 172, 174–176, 179–181, 187, 190, 193–197, 199, 200–202, 204–205, 207, 208–211, 213–215, 22–224, 227, 229

Parker Feierbach: 18, 30–31, 40–41, 50, 52–53, 55, 59–61, 62, 64–65, 69, 70–71, 77–80, 84, 87, 90, 95, 104, 116–117, 124–125, 128–139, 132–133, 136–138, 154–155, 157–158, 164, 169–171, 182–184, 188–189, 217–291, 221

Chelsea Kyle: 161, 167

Ethan Calabrese: 72–73, 126, 153

Alexandra Folino: 8–9

Tyler Joe: 28–29

Allie Holloway: 150–151

Michael Kleinberg: 28

Courtesy of Fiddlestix: 88–89

Courtesy of La Cantina: 151

231

Published by Hearst Home, an imprint of Hearst Books/Hearst Magazine Media, Inc.

Hearst Magazine Media, Inc.
300 West 57th Street
New York, NY 10019

Delish, Hearst Home, the Hearst Home logo, and Hearst Books are registered trademarks of Hearst Magazine Media, Inc.

For information about custom editions, special sales, premium and corporate purchases: hearst.com/magazines/hearst-books

Printed in China
ISBN 978-1-950785-15-5